WHAT WOULD YOU CHOOSE?

GO TO THE MOON OR THE DEEPEST OCEAN FLOOR?

PERILOUS PLACES

HELEN GREATHEAD

Gareth Stevens
PUBLISHING

Please visit our website, www.garethstevens.com.
For a free color catalog of all our high-quality books,
call toll free 1-800-542-2595 or fax 1-877-542-2596.

Cataloging-in-Publication Data

Names: Greathead, Helen.
Title: Perilous places / Helen Greathead.
Description: New York : Gareth Stevens Publishing, 2017. l Series: What would you choose?l Includes index.
Identifiers: ISBN 9781482461169 (pbk.) l ISBN 9781482461763 (library bound) l ISBN 9781482461176 (6 pack)
Subjects: LCSH: Adaptation (Biology)--Juvenile literature. l Extreme environments--Juvenile literature.
Classification: LCC QH546.G724 2017 l DDC 578.4'7--d23

Published in 2017 by Gareth Stevens Publishing
111 East 14th Street, Suite 349
New York, NY 10003

Copyright © 2017 Franklin Watts, a division of Hachette Children's Group

Series editor: Adrian Cole
Art direction: Peter Scoulding
Series designer: D. R. ink
Picture researcher: Diana Morris

CONTENTS

WOULD YOU CHOOSE

TO SLEEP ON A BED OF ICE IN SWEDEN, BE CHASED BY BULLS IN SPAIN OR JUMP OFF A BRIDGE AT A WATERFALL CALLED "SMOKE THAT THUNDERS"?

Perilous Places invites you to think carefully about which of the world's weirdest and most wonderful places you'd really like to visit – and how.

Read each question,

CONSIDER YOUR OPTIONS

check out the facts

see what your friends think (and what we chose) and then make YOUR choice.

TAKE A DIP IN DOMINICA'S BOILING LAKE ... OR JORDAN'S DEAD SEA ?

WE CHOSE

The Dead Sea. The saltiness of its water means no animals or plants survive there, but it's so buoyant you could float on your back while reading a book! The water in Dominica's Boiling Lake really does boil; red-hot molten rock beneath the lake bed heats it up. Take a dip here and you'll get a scalding.

Didn't you know?
You should always float on your back in the Dead Sea – the water tastes disgusting!

SPEND A SPOOKY NIGHT IN THE TOWER OF LONDON ... OR IN EDINBURGH CASTLE?

WE CHOSE

Edinburgh – it's scarier! The Tower of London is said to be haunted by Henry VIII's wives, two murdered princes and even a bear. Edinburgh Castle boasts ghostly pipers, a headless drummer and a phantom dog. Scientific tests showed that ten percent of ghostly Tower sightings couldn't be explained, while in Edinburgh unexplained things happened in nearly all of the places thought to be haunted.

GO TO THE DEEPEST OCEAN FLOOR... OR THE MOON?

THE FACTS

THE MARIANA TRENCH:
- is 6.8 miles (11 km) below sea level
- measures 42.9 miles (69 km) wide and 1,491 miles (2,400 km) long
- is deeper than Mount Everest is tall
- takes five hours to reach by submersible
- was formed when two of the Earth's tectonic plates collided

WHAT'S IT LIKE THAT DEEP UNDERWATER?

There's no sunlight, so it's gloomy and cold with temperatures just above freezing. Water pressure on the ocean floor is about 1,000 times greater than at sea level, but creatures such as sea cucumbers and shrimps do survive here.

HOW DO YOU GET THERE?

You'll need a special vehicle, such as the Deepsea Challenger, that resists the super-high water pressure. You'll be crammed into a pilot cockpit just 43 inches (109 cm) wide, with your knees bent as you spin slowly downwards.

WHAT'S IT LIKE ON THE MOON?

The surface is pockmarked with meteor craters, and covered with a lumpy powder made from rock and volcanic glass. Gravity is weaker here. There's no animal or plant life, and no air — but there is water.

DO PEOPLE STILL GO THERE?

The last moonwalk was back in 1972, but since water molecules were discovered there in 2009, different organizations have been working on rockets suitable for a return trip.

THE FACTS

THE MOON:

- is nearly 240,000 miles (386,242 km) away from Earth
- measures roughly 2,346 miles (3,476 km) across
- welcomed its first human visitors in 1969
- took three days to reach by Apollo spacecraft

AND FINALLY ...

Twelve people have walked on the surface of the Moon in total, but only three people have ever descended to the bottom of the Mariana Trench — and nobody has ever walked its ocean floor.

WE CHOSE

The Moon. Work is happening to get back up there, and anyone can go — if they can afford the $1.26 billion fare.

CAMP BY NESSIE'S LAKE IN SCOTLAND ... OR NEAR A DRAGON'S LAIR IN INDONESIA?

WE CHOSE

The monster lake — it's safer. The legend of the monster in Loch Ness dates back 600 years, but there's never really been a proper sighting. The large lizards — called dragons — on Komodo Island are real. Camping is not allowed there, in case the dragons enter your tent and attack.

TAKE AN ELEVATOR TO THE TOP OF BERLIN'S ROCKET-SHAPED TV TOWER ... OR BRATISLAVA'S UFO OUTLOOK TOWER?

WE CHOSE

The TV Tower (right). You'll whiz up it in just 40 seconds — five seconds faster than the UFO elevator — and its viewing deck rotates, showing off the whole city, while you stand and watch. The UFO may be Slovakia's building of the century (left), but it's less than one third the height of Berlin's tower.

JUMP OFF THE VICTORIA FALLS BRIDGE... OR PADDLE DOWN THE ZAMBEZI RIVER?

Didn't you know?
If you fall in, keep your legs up, so they don't get caught in rocks, and watch out for crocs!

From the Victoria Falls Bridge, across the Zambezi River at the border between Zimbabwe and Zambia, you'll jump 364 feet (111 m) down to the swirling, croc-infested waters below. Just before you reach the water, the bungee rope tied to your feet will spring you back up and you'll get an incredible, upside-down view of the largest waterfall in the world.

To paddle, climb into your raft just after the Victoria Falls (or *Mosi-oa-Tunya*, meaning "smoke that thunders"), and you'll be traveling through a deep gorge. You'll need to wear a helmet and a life jacket, and you'll only have a plastic paddle for steering. The scenery is stunning, with lush vegetation — all you have to worry about are the grade five rapids. (Eeeeeek!)

WE CHOSE

Jump! Bungee jumping isn't 100 percent safe, but once you've jumped, you can't do anything except admire the view ... and scream! There are more grade five rapids in this gorge (with names like the "Gnashing Jaws of Death"!) than anywhere else in the world and you will definitely fall in!

TAKE THE ROAD THROUGH THE CLOUD FOREST IN BOLIVIA ... OR ALONG AN ICY ALASKAN HIGHWAY?

THE FACTS

THE NORTH YUNGAS ROAD, BOLIVIA:
- is 43 miles (69 km) long
- leads from Bolivia's capital, La Paz, to the Amazon rain forest
- drops 11,482 feet (3,500 m) in 39 miles (63 km)
- is mostly only 10 feet (3 m) wide!

HOW EASY IS THE RIDE?

Not very. The road isn't much more than a dirt track, winding up a mountain. You'll need to check the weather, your tires and brakes. Year-round mists make visibility difficult and rain can cause waterfalls and mudslides that wash away the road.

SO WHY BOTHER?

For many years, locals had no choice. Today tourists challenge themselves to bike down! The scenery is breathtaking: the road starts at the top of an icy mountain, descends through lush green forest and finishes in fruit orchards and tropical heat.

Didn't you know?
You should give way to uphill traffic, and avoid landslips by not riding the road in the wet season.

Didn't you know? You should always give way to the big trucks that race up and down.

THIS IS A HIGHWAY, RIGHT?

Yep, but on the Dalton Highway you'll need to take plenty of food and warm clothing – the temperature can dip below -76° F (-60° C)! The road is a two-lane gravel track that twists and turns over steep hills. Watch out for avalanches and fast-changing weather.

SO WHY BOTHER?

Truck drivers don't have a choice. Their 18-wheel trucks take supplies to the workers on the Arctic oil wells. Tourists take the route for the scenery – snowy mountain ranges, rivers, forests – and the chance of spotting bears, rare birds or herds of caribou.

THE FACTS

THE DALTON HIGHWAY, ALASKA:
- is 414 miles (666 km) long
- has only one fuel stop
- leads to the sleepy town of Deadhorse – beyond the Arctic Circle
- takes over 14 hours to drive

AND FINALLY ...

These are two of the most dangerous roads in the world. The Dalton Highway averages 10 accidents and 1 death each year. The North Yungas Road now has a bypass; but around 26 vehicles still plunge 1,968 feet (600 m) over the edge each year, causing 100 deaths. Unsurprisingly its nickname is the "Death Road."

WE CHOSE

Take the ice road ... slowly and carefully!

VISIT NORTH SENTINEL ISLAND IN THE BAY OF BENGAL ... OR A HOMEMADE ISLAND ON LAKE TITICACA?

WE CHOSE

Lake Titicaca in South America. The Uros people on Lake Titicaca first built islands — using reeds, ropes and logs — to escape their Inca enemies. Today you're welcome to visit — for a small fee! The Sentinelese people have no contact with the outside world. Visit their island and they're likely to kill you!

FIND YOUR LUNCH IN THAILAND FLOATING IN A CANAL ... OR ON AN OLD RAILWAY LINE?

WE CHOSE

The canal. The wooden canoes on Bangkok's floating markets sell delicious treats, such as coconut pancakes. Food at the railway market is equally tasty, but the old track is still in use! Around three times a day, stallholders scrabble to move their wares before a train rattles right through the market.

WHAT WOULD YOU CHOOSE?

GET LOST IN A MAZE AT AN ITALIAN VILLA ... OR A MAZE ON A HAWAIIAN PINEAPPLE PLANTATION?

Didn't you know?
To find your way out of a maze, choose the left or right wall and follow it all the way around.

WE CHOSE

Italy's Villa Pisani. It has the hardest maze in the world. It's claimed that Napoleon Bonaparte once got lost there, and Adolf Hitler didn't dare enter, in case he couldn't get out. You're less likely to get lost in the Dole Plantation's pineapple, but with 2.5 miles (4 km) of paths, it does take the prize for being the largest maze in the world.

CRUISE ACROSS THE BERMUDA TRIANGLE ... OR STEER A CARGO SHIP ON THE SOUTH CHINA SEA?

WE CHOSE

Take the cruise. The Bermuda Triangle between Florida, Puerto Rico and Bermuda is famous for mysterious plane and ship disappearances, but statistics show it's no more dangerous than other busy ocean areas. Tropical storms and poorly kept cargo ships mean more accidents happen in the South China Sea than any other part of the ocean.

RUN WITH BULLS IN SPAIN ...
OR SUMMON UP DEAD
RELATIVES IN MEXICO?

THE FACTS

THE BULL RUN:

- is part of a nine-day religious festival held each year in Pamplona, Spain
- involves six bulls weighing up to 1,320 pounds (600 kg)
- only lasts a few minutes
- covers about a half mile (just under 1 km) of winding, cobbled streets
- attracts tens of thousands of spectators

SO WHAT DO YOU DO?

Each morning you'll gather with the crowds in front of the bulls' corral. After two rockets are fired the bulls are released onto the streets. The bulls surge through the crowds at up to 15.5 mph (25 km/h). You'll try to run ahead of them, jumping away when the bulls come close.

WHERE'S EVERYONE GOING?

To the bullring, where crowds of spectators are waiting to watch the bullfights.

IS IT DANGEROUS?

Absolutely! A bull's horns are sharp. Fifteen people have been killed since 1924.

Didn't you know? Taking selfies on the Pamplona bull run is illegal!

Didn't you know?
If the wind picks up, you're said to be witnessing the souls of the dead returning home.

THE FACTS

DAY OF THE DEAD IS:

- two days long, running from November 1 to November 2
- part of a week-long festival, ending on November 2
- a mixture of native Mexican tradition and Catholic religion
- celebrated all over Mexico
- best seen on the Mexican island of Janitzio

AND FINALLY ...

Most bulls die in the bullfight. In many parts of Spain, bullfighting has been banned because of its cruelty. The Day of the Dead is more about celebrating life than being miserable. There are games, music and even skull-shaped sweets!

WE CHOSE

The dead relatives – they're even said to bring you good luck!

SO WHAT HAPPENS AT DAY OF THE DEAD?

Families decorate a homemade altar. When the cemetery bell tolls at midnight, you'll walk down there with food, drink, candles and marigold flowers. You'll decorate the graves, offer the food to your departed loved ones, pray, sing and tell stories until dawn.

WHY DO IT?

It's said that, at this time, the dead are allowed to come back and visit the living. The offerings are supposed to keep their relatives happy.

CLIMB HAWAII'S STAIRWAY TO HEAVEN ... OR LEAN OVER NEW ZEALAND'S CRATERS OF THE MOON?

WE CHOSE

Craters of the Moon. This field of bubbling, sulfurous mud created by underground geothermal activity is near Taupo, New Zealand. It feels like you're on another planet! The Stairway to Heaven is a set of 4,000 treacherous steps into the Koolau Mountain Range. The route was officially closed in 1987, but that doesn't stop hikers risking their lives to climb it.

GO TO SCHOOL BY CABLE CAR IN CHINA ... OR OVER A TREE BRIDGE IN NORTHEAST INDIA?

WE CHOSE

The tree bridge. Traveling by cable car in Guizhou Province, China, means schoolchildren avoid a 5-hour journey up and down a mountain. However, they're crossing a valley that's hundreds of feet deep. India's Ficus elastica tree has really strong roots that can be trained to grow straight across a river. It takes about 15 years for a tree bridge to grow, but then they can hold up to 50 people at once and last 500 years.

LIVE IN GARBAGE CITY ... OR AT THE BASE OF AN ACTIVE VOLCANO?

Manshiett Naser, or "Garbage City," receives 15,432 tons (14,000 mt) of garbage produced each day in Cairo, Egypt. Once there, it's sorted by the Zabaleen people, who recycle the waste, selling anything of value. Not surprisingly, Garbage City smells of rotting garbage, animal poop and burning plastic.

A volcanic eruption on the Japanese island of Miyake-Jima meant it had to be completely evacuated in 2000. Some residents were allowed back in 2005, but others had to wait until 2011! There's a permanent smell of rotten eggs here, and you're advised to carry a gas mask at all times.

WE CHOSE

Garbage City. It doesn't smell sweet, but life could improve soon, as the government plans to make the Zabaleen's work official, giving them uniforms and vehicles. Parts of Miyake-Jima will always be off-limits. Poisonous gases coming from the volcano mean no one under 19 years of age can live there and all residents need regular health checks.

DIVE THE GREAT BARRIER REEF ...
OR THE WRECK OF THE *TITANIC*?

THE FACTS

THE GREAT BARRIER REEF:
- is over 1,242 miles (2,000 km) long
- lies in the Pacific Ocean, off the northeastern coast of Australia
- is made up of thousands of smaller reefs
- grows by 0.5 inch (1.3 cm) a year
- is millions of years old

Didn't you know?
Australia's jellyfish season runs from around November to June. During this time it's best to cover up completely with a stinger suit.

WHAT ELSE IS SPECIAL ABOUT IT?

It's the largest living structure on Earth. You might spot over 300 species of coral, 2,000 species of fish, plus sea turtles, sharks and dolphins. It's fabulously colorful, but it's also in trouble.

WHAT'S THE PROBLEM?

Tropical storms are destroying the coral, warmer waters are causing coral bleaching and, while some reef animals are struggling to survive, others, like the crown-of-thorns starfish that eats the reef, are thriving.

WHAT WAS SO SPECIAL ABOUT THE RMS *TITANIC*?

Before it sank in 1912, the *Titanic* was the largest moving object ever built, and the most luxurious. Like a floating city ten decks high, it had a gym, squash courts, a hospital and the first-ever ship's swimming pool. However, 100 years underwater have taken their toll.

WHAT'S HAPPENED TO IT?

The wreck of the ship was only discovered in 1985. Some incredible features were still intact, but the wooden decks had already rotted away and rust was eating up the steel bodywork.

THE FACTS

THE RMS *TITANIC*:
- **set out on its maiden voyage on April 10, 1912**
- **sailed from Southampton, UK for New York carrying 2,200 people**
- **was considered unsinkable**
- **crashed into an iceberg on April 10, 1912 and sank, killing over 1,500 people**

AND FINALLY ...

The waters around the Great Barrier Reef are warm all year round, and you don't have to dive deep to find it. The RMS Titanic lies 2.5 miles (4 km) below, in the cooler North Atlantic Ocean. You'd have to dive down in a submersible, plus you still can't get inside. There's lots of work being done to protect the reef, but the Titanic will probably be left to rot.

WE CHOSE

The reef while it's teeming with life, not the underwater graveyard.

TITANIC
The World's
Largest Liner
WHITE STAR LINE
SOUTHAMPTON – NEW YORK
VIA CHERBOURG & QUEENSTOWN

GROW UP IN ROMANIA ...
OR THE NETHERLANDS?

AMSTERDAM

BUCHAREST

WE CHOSE

The Netherlands. According to a 2013 report by children's charity, UNICEF, the Netherlands came first in a league of 29 developed countries. Romania was ranked last. Happiness was judged on where children lived and learned, whether they were safe, healthy, wealthy, and whether they ate breakfast in the morning.

FLOAT THROUGH THE BLUE GROTTO OF CAPRI ...
OR WAITOMO GLOWWORM CAVES IN NEW ZEALAND?

WE CHOSE

Waitomo. You can spend an hour floating around the Waitomo Caves (right). They twinkle with glowworms, and Waitomo's huge cathedral cave also hosts music concerts! When the sun lights the Blue Grotto its waters turn a shimmering turquoise color (below), and your boatman may burst into song. Enjoy it while you can — the boat only stays inside for five minutes.

WHAT WOULD YOU CHOOSE?

WATCH THE CHANGING OF THE GUARD IN ATHENS, GREECE ... OR THE CLOSING OF THE INDIA—PAKISTAN BORDER AT WAGAH?

The Greek "Evzone" soldiers are tall and strong, so the uniform of tasseled hat and garters, cotton minikilt and hobnailed clogs with pompoms on the toes is surprising! The changing of the guard ceremony at the Tomb of the Unknown Soldier looks a bit like a slow-motion clog dance.

Soldiers on either side of the Wagah border gate wear plain uniforms dressed up with colored sashes and fancy fans on their turbans. The ceremony is full of high-kicking, knee-raising and top-speed marching. It's a show of mock aggression that ends with a handshake between two rival guards, and the closing of the gate.

WE CHOSE

The border ceremony at Wagah. While the Greek display attracts the tourists (left), the border closure draws thousands of locals from India and Pakistan (below) for an unforgettable show. The guards on each side bellow, stamp and thumb wave (to outdo their rivals) while the crowds chant wildly for their respective country.

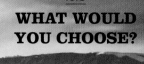

CLIMB THE EARTH'S TALLEST MOUNTAIN ... OR THE WORLD'S HIGHEST PEAK?

THE FACTS

KILIMANJARO:

- is the Earth's tallest freestanding mountain, at 19,340 feet* (5,895 m*)
- was first successfully climbed in 1889
- lies in Tanzania, East Africa
- is actually a volcano that hasn't erupted for 360,000 years!

Didn't you know?
You should climb slowly. If you start to suffer headaches, dizziness and sickness (symptoms of altitude sickness), descend to a lower altitude.

WHAT'S KILIMANJARO LIKE?

It's full of contrasts. You'll set off in boiling heat, trek through grasslands, cloud and forest, to alpine desert, snow and temperatures as low as 0° F (-18° C)! Some plants growing here don't exist anywhere else in the world.

HOW HARD IS THE CLIMB?

Not too bad, but you'll need to be fit — the final stretch is a killer! You'll start at midnight to get up to the peak, walking steeply uphill all the way, with only 15 minutes at the summit. But you'll have local guides to carry your luggage, set up your tent, cook and even bring you a cup of tea in the morning.

* Mauna Kea is actually taller, if you include the part of it below sea level.

WHAT WOULD YOU CHOOSE?

WHAT'S EVEREST LIKE?

At base camp you're already 17,598 feet (5,364 m) above sea level and there's snow all year round. You'll cross glaciers and deadly crevasses by ladder and just before the summit, there's the treacherous "Death Zone." Even on the warmest day, the summit temperature will be 0° F (-18° C) — brrrrrrrrr!

HOW HARD IS THE CLIMB?

Very tough! You'll need to train for two years and pack specialist clothing and equipment — harnesses, ropes, ice picks, bottled oxygen.... Luckily, Sherpa guides will carry most of the supplies for you.

THE FACTS

EVEREST:
- is the highest peak of the Himalaya mountain range, and at 29,029 feet (8,848 m) above sea level, it's also the highest peak in the world
- was first successfully climbed in 1953
- lies in two countries, Tibet and Nepal

AND FINALLY ...

35,000 people attempt the 5-day to 9-day climb up Kilimanjaro each year, and roughly 10–15 die trying. It takes at least 40 days to climb Everest and the death rate here is roughly 1 in 27. Dead bodies litter the route! On fine days there are "traffic jams" of people waiting to get to the top and there's garbage everywhere, from empty oxygen bottles to frozen human poop!

WE CHOSE

Kilimanjaro. At busy times Everest is just too crowded!

Didn't you know?
As well as altitude sickness, climbers prepare for frostbite, hypothermia, broken bones (if they fall), extreme sunburn and avalanches.

SLEEP ON A BED OF ICE IN SWEDEN ... OR HANGING FROM A TREE IN GERMANY?

In Sweden's ice hotel (below), rooms, sculptures and beds are cut from ice. You'll take a "survival course" before snuggling down in thermal undies, a hat and an Arctic sleeping bag. The ice beds are covered with reindeer skins and they promise the temperature won't dip below 23° F (-5° C)!

In Germany, the tree you'll be dangling from is a giant beech and the views 20 feet (6 m) up are spectacular. You'll take a safety course before climbing the rope to your "portaledge" (left), and you'll have to wear a harness all night, along with all your clothes.

WE CHOSE

The ice bed. Slip out of your ice bed and you won't fall far. The ice hotel rooms are luxurious, many designed by artists; some even have en suite toilets! The portaledge has just enough room for two. When the wind sways it you'll worry about falling out, and if you need to poop in the night you'll have to climb down a rope in the dark.

KISS THE BLARNEY STONE IN IRELAND ...
OR SPEAK TO THE ORACLE AT DELPHI, GREECE?

Legends say the Blarney Stone — embedded high up in a wall of Blarney Castle — may have come from Scotland, or from the Crusades. They also say that kissing the "enchanted" stone will give you the gift of persuasive speech. That's why millions of people have willingly dangled over the edge of the castle!

Ancient Greeks believed the Oracle at Delphi was the center of the world. From 1200 BC, they came here to discover their fortunes. A priestess, who had breathed in magical vapors from the waters beneath the temple, would fall into a trance and deliver cryptic messages from the great god Apollo himself.

WE CHOSE

Kiss the stone. Geologists found that the Blarney Stone was just a local, Irish rock — but they haven't proved it wasn't enchanted! The oracle apparently lost its power in the 4th century AD, and those vapors turned out to be ethylene gas.

WALK THROUGH ARGENTINA'S FOSSIL FOREST ... OR THE RED FOREST OF CHERNOBYL?

About 150 million years ago, Jaramillo Forest, in Argentina, was full of monkey puzzle trees. When a massive volcanic eruption covered it in lava and ash, its 1,000-year-old trees fell and gradually turned to rock. At 115 feet (35 m) long and 10 feet (3 m) wide, some of these fossil trees are the largest of their kind in the world.

In 1986 Ukraine's Chernobyl Nuclear Plant suffered the world's worst-ever nuclear disaster. It killed people, animals and plants, and the area was abandoned. Many trees turned a strange red-brown color, then died. Experts assumed nothing could live here, but 30 years later some trees are still growing.

WE CHOSE

The Jaramillo Forest. In Argentina you can see where minerals have turned some tree trunks vivid rainbow colors – plus, you don't have to wear a radiation suit to see them. Trees may be growing in Chernobyl, but experts say the high radiation levels mean it will not be safe for 20,000 years!

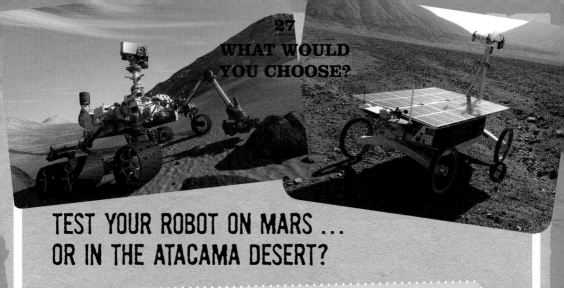

TEST YOUR ROBOT ON MARS ... OR IN THE ATACAMA DESERT?

WE CHOSE

The Atacama Desert in South America. It's the driest place on Earth, with rain falling once every ten years! Humans haven't set foot on Mars yet, but conditions in parts of the Atacama are said to be very similar. That's why NASA tests its robot rovers there, before landing them on Mars to search for signs of life.

DRESS AS A BEAR IN BACAU, ROMANIA ... OR THROW STUFF OUT OF THE WINDOW IN NAPLES, ITALY?

WE CHOSE

Bacau, Romania. Here, people dance through the streets in bear costumes on New Year's Eve to drive away evil spirits. In Naples, Italy, midnight on New Year's Eve is the time to literally fling anything you don't want — pots, pans, even fridges — out of the window! So watch your head, because accidents do happen.

SEE INSIDE THE GREAT PYRAMID AT GIZA, EGYPT ... OR CLIMB THE STEPS TO THE TOP OF MEXICO'S PYRAMID OF THE SUN?

THE FACTS

THE GREAT PYRAMID:
- is the largest pyramid ever built
- was completed in around 2550 BC
- measured 755 feet (230 m) along each side
- contains around 2.3 million stone blocks that (on average) weigh 2.4 tons (2.2 mt) each
- lies north of Cairo, Egypt, on the west bank of the Nile River

WHAT WAS THE PYRAMID AT GIZA BUILT FOR?

It was built as a tomb where the Egyptian Pharaoh Khufu's mummified body would be laid to rest, with food, wealth and possessions to help him travel on to the afterlife.

WHAT'S IT LIKE INSIDE?

Not great if you're scared of small spaces, especially when it's busy. The tomb was robbed of its contents centuries ago and there are no paintings on the walls. From the entrance you head straight down a seriously steep, dark, narrow passage leading to one of three chambers. The pharaoh's chamber contains a granite sarcophagus.

Didn't you know?
Today the Great Pyramid looks bumpy, but when it was first built it had an outer layer of polished white limestone.

WHAT WAS THE PYRAMID OF THE SUN BUILT FOR?

It was probably a tomb for a great ruler — but experts aren't sure who. Chambers underneath the pyramid show signs of rituals taking place and experts still hope to find human remains here. The Aztecs discovered the pyramid in the 1300s and believed it was the birthplace of the Sun.

WHAT'S IT LIKE AT THE TOP?

You'll need a head for heights. The 248 steps are steep! There's no sign of the temple that was once at the top, but you can see along the 2.5-mile (4 km) Avenue of the Dead, across the whole of Teotihuacán and to the mountains beyond.

THE FACTS

THE PYRAMID OF THE SUN:

- was one of the largest structures in the Americas
- measures 730 feet (222.5 m) along each side
- was built in around AD 100, using volcanic stone, brick and rubble
- weighs around 3 million tons (2.7 million mt)
- lies in the ancient, ruined city of Teotihuacán, northeast of Mexico City

AND FINALLY ...

Both pyramids are spectacular, but the Great Pyramid is almost twice as big as the Sun Pyramid. It was the tallest structure on Earth for around 4,000 years and is roughly 2,600 years older. More mysterious passages may yet be revealed inside the Great Pyramid, while the Sun Pyramid is filled with rubble and scientists say it could collapse very soon!

WE CHOSE

The Great Pyramid — it's the only one of the Seven Wonders of the Ancient World that is still standing.

TOUR THE PARIS SEWERS ... OR THE PARIS CATACOMBS?

WE CHOSE

The sewers. Over 62 miles (100 km) of catacomb tunnels hold the skeletons of around 6 million long-dead Parisians (bottom right), but without name tags no one knows who the bones belonged to. There are 1,304 miles (2,100 km) of tunnels in the sewers (top), each labeled to correspond with the city street above. The outflow from each building even has a house number!

VISIT THE MUSEUM OF PARASITES IN JAPAN ... OR THE MUSEUM OF BROKEN RELATIONSHIPS IN ZAGREB, CROATIA?

WE CHOSE

Zagreb. The museum began as a touring exhibition, using stories and objects donated by ex-girlfriends and ex-boyfriends. The idea caught on and the crowds, and donations, just keep coming. So, while looking at 300 tiny dead creatures that live on humans and other animals in Japan is fascinating (you can see some eyelash mites on the top left), Zagreb's museum wins the popularity contest.

WHAT WOULD
YOU CHOOSE?

GLOSSARY

altar — The table in a Christian church where wine and bread are blessed.

altitude sickness — Illness caused from a change in altitude or height.

Apollo — The name of the US space program, and also the ancient Greek god.

avalanches — Masses of snow, ice and rock falling very quickly down a mountainside.

buoyant — Able to keep afloat.

caribou — Reindeer.

corral — An enclosure or pen for animals.

developed countries — Nations that are industrialized and wealthy.

ethylene gas — A colorless gas produced by plants, which ripens fruits.

geothermal activity — Conditions or events produced by the internal heat of the Earth, such as warm ground and hot pools.

gorge — A narrow valley between mountains.

grade five rapids — Where a river or rapid has been given a grade five rating against the International Scale of River Difficulty; grade six being the most difficult and dangerous.

gravity — A force that attracts a body or thing to the center of a planet.

hypothermia — A condition where body temperature is too low.

meteor crater — A basin-shaped hole in the surface of a planet where a lump of space rock, called a meteor, has crashed.

nuclear disaster — Where hazardous material is released into the environment when an accident occurs at a nuclear power plant.

sarcophagus — A container for a dead body, often displayed aboveground.

Seven Wonders of the Ancient World — Seven amazing pieces of art or buildings created during ancient times.

Sherpa — A group of people who live in Nepal.

statistics — A fact taken from a large study of information.

submersible — A small vehicle designed to move underwater.

sulfurous — Containing sulfur, which is an acidic chemical.

summit — The top of a mountain or hill.

tectonic plates — Large sections or plates that make up the Earth's outer surface.

volcanic glass — A type of glass made from the cooling of lava from a volcano.

WEBSITES

A special series of photographs shows how the *Titanic* looks today, in its resting place in the North Atlantic: **http://ngm. nationalgeographic.com/2012/04/titanic/ titanic-photography**

Here's the story of the Waitomo Caves: **http:// www.newzealand.com/int/article/the- underground-glories-of-waitomo-roadside- stories/**

Experience the Ice Hotel here: **http://www. icehotel.com**

INDEX